Amelia
A to Z

By Rob and Kim Hicks

Illustrated by Sharon Bolton-Eells

Island Media Publishing, LLC
120 N. 15th St.
Fernandina Beach, FL 32034
www.islandmediapublishing.com
Printed in China

ISBN 978-0-9829908-0-3
Library of Congress 2010936737

Island Media Publishing, LLC

For Burgess who loved this island and for Clay who surely will.
Rob and Kim Hicks

To my family for always being there with love and support.
Sharon Bolton-Eells

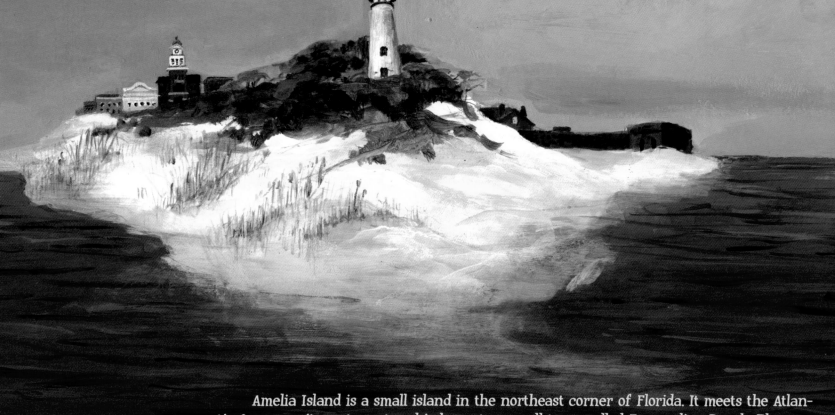

A is for Amelia and Amelia A to Z.
It's a place that's very small but full of history.
Amelia is an island within the Atlantic's reach.
It's home to a little town called Fernandina Beach.

Amelia Island is a small island in the northeast corner of Florida. It meets the Atlantic Ocean on its east coast and is home to a small town called Fernandina Beach. The island is roughly thirteen miles long and two miles wide with a population of around 20,000 people.

Today, it is perhaps best known as a tourist destination with outstanding beaches and resorts, but other industries such as fishing and paper manufacturing are very important as well. Amelia is also home to a rich history that began 4,000 years ago when Timucuan Indians first settled the area.

B is for border, Amelia's imaginary line
that separates Georgia from the Florida sunshine.
The border was really important in the days of ole
when it separated the U.S. from Florida's foreign control.

Amelia Island is in Florida but is very close to Georgia. Georgia is just to the north of Amelia Island, across the water from Fort Clinch. That body of water is called the Cumberland Sound and it separates Amelia Island from Cumberland Island. It also represents the border, or imaginary line, that separates the two states. A long time ago, Florida wasn't part of the United States but Georgia was. Then, Florida belonged to Spain. Amelia Island was very important because it was the main town that separated these two countries. Some people used Amelia Island as a base for smuggling things that were illegal into the United States. A lot of dangerous visitors came to Amelia Island during this time, even pirates!

C is for Centre, the town's most famous street.
It was home to our first businesses and a place for people to meet.
Today, the street is part of what's commonly called downtown
where tourists, shopping, and dining are likely to be found.

In the mid 1800s, Centre Street was constructed on Amelia Island with the railroad depot and docks at the end of the street. Here, lumber, cotton, and other goods that were grown in the middle of Florida were brought by the railroads to Amelia Island where they were placed on large ships and delivered around the world.

The railroad and docks were so important, many shops and businesses soon opened along the street. Today, Centre Street is still a very busy place. Many shops, offices, and restaurants can be found there, and the area is a favorite among tourists.

D is for Duncan Clinch, whose name is on the fort
rising up among the dunes, along the northern shore.
The fort is from the Civil War but never saw a fight.
Southern troops abandoned it against the Northern might.

Fort Clinch was named in honor of Duncan Lamont Clinch. He served as a general during the Seminole Wars. These wars did not have a big impact on Amelia Island but did throughout the rest of Florida.

Construction began on the fort in 1842, but it took a long time to finish. Twenty years later, during the Civil War, the Confederacy was in control of the unfinished fort. However, Union forces moved through Georgia and came across the Cumberland Sound toward Fort Clinch. The Southern forces didn't think they could defend the fort, so they surrendered it before a battle began. For the rest of the war, the Northern forces occupied Fort Clinch. Since there were no Civil War battles on Amelia Island, the soldiers got bored and finally put the finishing touches on the fort. Afterward, it was ignored and was covered by sand from the beach. In 1935, it was restored and became a state park.

E is for all eight flags Amelia gets to claim.
That's the most in all the country so it gave us our nickname.
French, Spanish, and English are some of the flags that flew.
Others like the Patriots lasted just a day or two.

France was the first country to raise its flag over Amelia Island in 1562. However, Spain already controlled much of Florida and wanted possession of the island. The Spanish soon overpowered the French and raised their own flag. War continued in the New World, and, as a result of the French and Indian War, the British took Amelia Island but later had to give it back to Spain.

In 1812, local planters revolted against the Spanish and successfully captured the island. They called themselves the Patriots and raised their own flag over Amelia. One day later they gave the island to the United States. However, Spain demanded the island be given back to them.

Spain had a hard time keeping control of things in Florida, and in 1817 a man name Gregor MacGregor captured the island and tried to create his own country. He raised the Green Cross of Florida over Amelia, but he could not afford to keep control. About a month later a young man named Luis Aury arrived with a little money. He was able to raise his own flag over Amelia. That flag is called the Mexican Rebel Flag.

Soon, Aury was forced to give Amelia Island to the United States. Later, in 1845, Florida officially became part of the United States. However, after the Civil War began Florida joined the Confederacy and the island's eighth flag was raised. After the war, Florida rejoined the Union and the American flag has flown ever since.

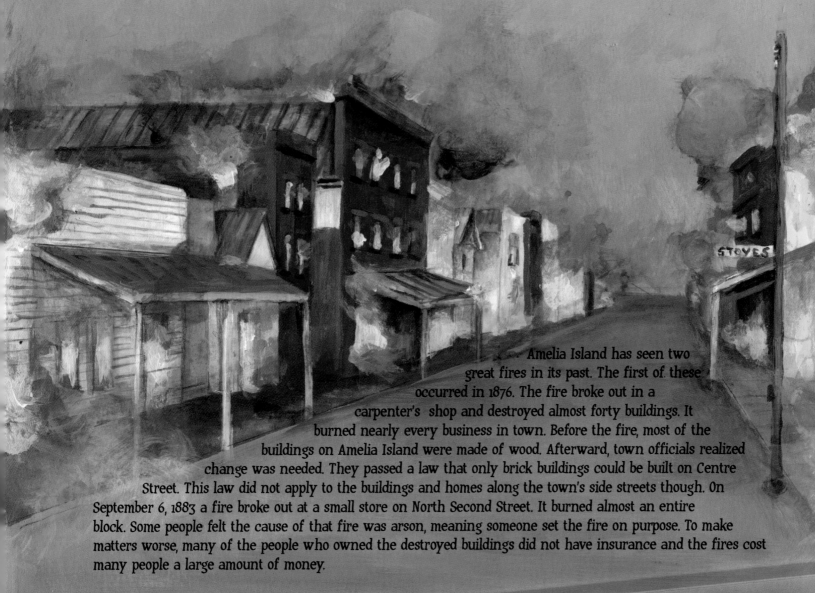

F is for the great fire of 1876
that caused the wooden buildings to burn up really quick.
By law, brick replaced wood along old Centre Street,
but a fire destroyed a side road in 1883.

Amelia Island has seen two great fires in its past. The first of these occurred in 1876. The fire broke out in a carpenter's shop and destroyed almost forty buildings. It burned nearly every business in town. Before the fire, most of the buildings on Amelia Island were made of wood. Afterward, town officials realized change was needed. They passed a law that only brick buildings could be built on Centre Street. This law did not apply to the buildings and homes along the town's side streets though. On September 6, 1883 a fire broke out at a small store on North Second Street. It burned almost an entire block. Some people felt the cause of that fire was arson, meaning someone set the fire on purpose. To make matters worse, many of the people who owned the destroyed buildings did not have insurance and the fires cost many people a large amount of money.

G is for golf, one of the sports played
on Amelia Island each and every day.
Many of the courses are found at the resorts
which are also home to world-class tennis courts.

Amelia Island is full of sporting opportunities. It features over 100 holes of golf. Many of these holes were designed by the best known golf course designers in the world. Some of these courses are part of the Omni Amelia Island Plantation and the Ritz-Carlton, Amelia Island. The resorts also have wonderful tennis facilities that have hosted professional tournaments. Many tourists come to Amelia to enjoy these golf courses and tennis courts.

There are other activities to participate in on Amelia Island. Fishing has always been popular. There are several well-worn bike trails at the Omni Amelia Island Plantation, Fort Clinch, and at the Egan's Creek Greenway. Some people like to take jogs or leisurely strolls along these same trails or on the beach. Swimming is another popular form of recreation, be it in the ocean or in the many pools on the island. Amelia Island truly is a sportsman's paradise.

H is for hurricane, like the one in 1898.
It destroyed many houses and is still our worst to date.
The storm grew very powerful from the ocean water's heat.
The rising waters that resulted washed a boat into the street.

All Atlantic Ocean hurricanes start as a tropical wave moving off the coast of Africa during the warmer months. As the tropical wave feeds off the warm waters of the ocean, it strengthens. If conditions are just right and the water temperature is warm enough, the storm can gain tremendous wind and rain potential. A hurricane is rated on how fast its winds are moving. A category one hurricane has winds that are as fast as 74 miles per hour. The strongest hurricanes are rated as a category five and can have winds that can be faster than 155 miles per hour.

In 1898, a powerful hurricane struck just north of Amelia Island. The National Weather Service has said the storm was probably a category four hurricane so its winds were at least 131 miles per hour. The storm destroyed almost all of the buildings on Amelia Island's beaches and caused lots of damage along Centre Street. A boat was even washed several blocks inland.

I is for island. Amelia is surrounded on each side
by water that flows in and out according to the tide.
The island is a barrier for the mainland and the marsh,
protecting them from wind and waves that can be extremely harsh.

AMELIA RIVER

NASSAU SOUND

ATLANTIC OCEAN

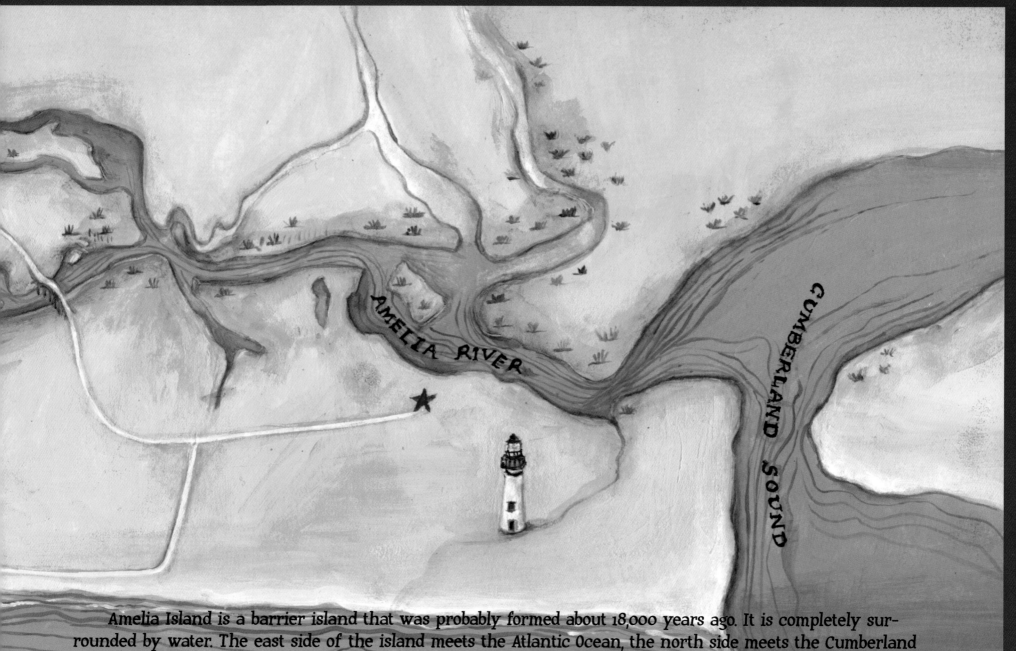

Amelia Island is a barrier island that was probably formed about 18,000 years ago. It is completely surrounded by water. The east side of the island meets the Atlantic Ocean, the north side meets the Cumberland Sound, the west side meets the Amelia River, and the south side meets the Nassau Sound.

A barrier island's main function is to protect the mainland from powerful waves and winds caused by hurricanes and other strong storms. It also provides a habitat for the many animals and insects that live around the island. Many of these animals depend on the tides that rise and fall from the gravitational pull of the sun and moon.

J is for jetty, a line of stone and rock
that keeps the river's opening from becoming blocked.
Deep water is needed for boats and submarines
so this rocky barrier keeps our channel clean.

The jetty at Amelia Island's north end is nothing more than a long line of large stones and rocks. The Amelia Island Jetty was built during the 1880s. Another jetty was built on the southern tip of Cumberland Island. Together, these jetties form a channel and keep the entrance of the Cumberland Sound and the St. Mary's River open. They help to keep sand and other sediment from drifting into the channel and blocking it. They also help to permanently mark the opening of Cumberland Sound. Without them the exact location of the channel could shift over the course of a long period of time and destroy buildings like Fort Clinch.

This is especially important for the large cargo ships that come into the port of Fernandina Beach and the submarines stationed at Kings Bay in Georgia. Both of these need the channel to be extra deep, or they could risk running aground.

K is for kingfish, one of many that are caught
in Amelia's waters from a dinghy, dock, or yacht.
Some of the other creatures that just might be biting
are sharks, drum, and redfish--grouper, rays, and whiting.

Since Amelia Island is surrounded by water, many opportunities for fishing abound. Some people like to fish right off the beach, while others prefer to fish from the marsh or in Egan's Creek. The island also has a group of charter boat captains who are paid to take people fishing. Charter boat captains often take their passengers out in to the Atlantic Ocean off Amelia's shores where some larger fish like sharks and barracudas are caught.

The annual kingfish tournament is a very popular event for many area fishermen. However, there are lots of others fish that can be caught around Amelia Island including mahi mahi, wahoo, tarpon, king mackerel, cobia, amber-jack, red snapper, and sailfish.

L is for Abraham Lewis, founder of American Beach,
a business man from Jacksonville who needed a retreat-
a place to rest and relax, in spite of segregation,
where African-Americans could take a beach vacation.

Abraham Lincoln Lewis founded the Afro-American Life Insurance Company in Jacksonville in 1901. He eventually became president of the company and the first black millionaire in the state of Florida. Lewis made many large donations to area black colleges.

Despite all of his successes, he still faced a lot of discrimination as an African-American in the South. African-Americans were forced to attend different schools and to use different bathrooms than the ones white people used. They were also not allowed to go to the same beaches to enjoy themselves like the white people. Lewis wanted a place where his friends and family could go to relax to enjoy the beach. He found some ocean-front land for sale near the south end of Amelia Island and bought it. On this land he founded America Beach. A community was soon built there, and African-Americans finally had a place of their own where they could enjoy the ocean. It was so popular that it used to be one of the busiest beaches in Florida.

M is for marsh, where land and water combine
to form a soggy habitat where many animals dine.
The marsh has many plants growing in its waters
which contribute to the food chain of crabs, fish, and otters.

Around Amelia Island, the marsh is the area where the land blends into the inland waterways. Most of Amelia's marshes feature salt water with lots of grass growing around the area. As these grasses die, they decompose and give the marsh water its dark appearance. The decomposing grasses also contribute to the thick black mud found around the marsh.

The marsh is a very important habitat for many animals. The grasses serve as a food source and shelter for a variety of animals. Some species prefer to eat the animals that feed on the grasses. When visiting Amelia's marshes, it's easy to see some of the many animals that feed, live, or even breed there. Some of the animals to watch for include manatees, alligators, otters, raccoons, bobcats, fiddler crabs, and various other insects, birds, and fish.

N is for the nests turtles dig on summer nights
on Amelia's beaches and fill with spheres of white.
Mother turtle was born on this same beach, many years ago.
Her children will lay their own eggs here in twenty years or so.

The loggerhead and green turtle are the two species of turtles most commonly known to lay their eggs on the beaches of Amelia Island. Between May and October these turtles crawl out of the Atlantic Ocean and onto the beach. Once there, they dig a hole in the sand and lay around 115 eggs. Then they bury their eggs in the sand and return to the ocean. About 60 days later, the baby turtles hatch from the eggs and emerge from the sand. They quickly scamper back to the ocean where they spend the rest of their lives. About 20 years later when the turtles are ready to lay their own eggs, they'll return to the same beach where they were born to dig their nests.

Unfortunately, many of the baby turtles do not survive to dig their own nests. Many turtle nests are destroyed by raccoons, dogs running loose on the beach, or people. Lights from houses along the beach confuse the baby turtles that are looking for the moon to guide them to the ocean. For the baby turtles that do make it to the ocean, there are many predators waiting for them there. Some local residents help the baby turtles survive by joining a sea turtle watch group that finds the nests along the beach and marks them for protection.

O is for Old Town, Fernandina's original place.
A mission and a fort once occupied this space.
But the town would have to move to a more suitable location
to better meet the needs of the coming railroad station.

When the Spanish first occupied Amelia Island they built a mission to the Timucuan Indians at the site of present-day Old Town. In 1811, a town was platted there and named Fernandina. Fort San Carlos was soon built at Old Town to fortify the Spanish defenses. A portion of that fort can still be seen, but all that remains is a low row of bricks.

When it was decided to build a railroad station on Amelia Island, Old Town was in a bad location. The town sat across a marshy area from where the trains would have to travel, so it was decided that the whole town would move a little farther south to an area known as the Mattair-Fernandez estate. The site of the estate is now downtown Fernandina Beach and Centre Street.

P is for the paper mills, where each and every day
trees are turned to paper and workers earn their pay.
So when visitors ask, "What smells so funny?"
Locals often reply, "That's the smell of money."

During the 1930s the people of Amelia Island had fallen on hard times as much of Fernandina's business had moved to larger cities farther south. A new industry was needed to provide jobs. The city began looking for new businesses to bring to town and finally convinced two paper manufacturers to build mills here.

Today Smurfit-Stone Container and Rayonier still produce paper on the island at these mills. The Smurfit-Stone Container mill makes a product similar to cardboard. The Rayonier mill makes a thickening product from trees that goes in everything from make-up to ice cream. The process the mills use to make their products can sometimes release an unpleasant smell. However, for the locals that depend on the jobs the mills create, putting up with a little odor is worth it.

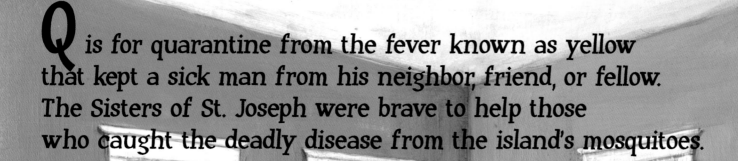

Q is for quarantine from the fever known as yellow
that kept a sick man from his neighbor, friend, or fellow.
The Sisters of St. Joseph were brave to help those
who caught the deadly disease from the island's mosquitoes.

In 1877, a wave of yellow fever broke out on Amelia Island. Yellow Fever is a deadly disease that is transmitted by mosquitoes. Fortunately, the disease is very rare in America today. It was quite common in the south during the warm summer months of the 1800s though.

When the disease broke out on Amelia Island, little was known about its cause or how to cure it. The most commonly used solution was quarantine, which is the process of separating sick people from healthy people. When quarantine orders were issued in Fernandina, the sick still needed someone to care for them. Nuns from the Catholic Church known as the Sisters of St. Joseph took on this dangerous mission. They helped quarantined fever victims during a very rough time. Sadly, two of the nuns caught yellow fever and died from the disease during their mission.

R is for Amelia's restaurants and resorts

R is for Amelia's restaurants and resorts
bringing tourists and visitors for fun of all sorts.
The resorts host big events or just let the tourists relax.
The restaurants serve all tastes, from gourmet meals to simple snacks.

Amelia Island is a popular destination for many people from all over the world. The Omni Amelia Island Plantation was constructed as a large golf and tennis resort in the 1970s. The Ritz-Carlton, Amelia Island came to town in the early 1990s. Many corporations like to hold conventions or retreats at these resorts. Their employees and their families can enjoy the sun and surf or spend their time playing golf or tennis. Other people are just looking for a place to relax.

The island is also home to lots of outstanding restaurants. Many restaurant-goers are looking for delicious seafood, and Amelia has lots of restaurants that serve fresh locally caught shrimp and fish. With so many great places to eat, it's hard to pick a favorite.

S is for shrimp, a crustacean of the sea.
Amelia is the birthplace of the shrimping industry.
The techniques that were invented here are used even still
by shrimpers around the world with nets they wish to fill.

Shrimp are small crustaceans that live in the ocean. When they are very young, they live close to the surface. As they grow, they move to the ocean floor where they scavenge for food. By the early 1900s the waters around the island were known to be full of shrimp. Many families came to take advantage of the bounty. Over time, several important changes were made in the way shrimp were caught. Local shrimpers started using boats with engines instead of those with sails so they could shrimp farther out. A device called the otter trawl allowed the shrimpers to drag their nets along the bottom of deeper water. These new techniques that were pioneered around Amelia Island made shrimping much easier and are still used around the world today.

T is for the Timucuan Indians who lived here long before.

They grew crops and gathered shellfish from Amelia's marshy shore.
The Timucua were a notable tribe adorned with high hairdos.
They also covered their bodies with elaborate tattoos.

The Timucuan Indians were the first people to live on Amelia Island. They came to the island around 4000 years ago and named it Napoyca. They covered their bodies with large tattoos using ink from plants found on the island. They also wore their hair pulled up high on their heads. The Indians grew many crops on the island and hunted the native animals.

The Timucua also enjoyed oysters. Usually, they ate the oysters as soon as they found them in the marsh then threw their shells on the ground. Over thousands of years, this made some big piles of shells. These piles, called middens, can still be seen today and often contain other Timucuan pottery and arrow heads.

U is for the German U-boats from the Second World War
waiting to attack the ships and towns all along the Atlantic's shore.
So Amelia had some volunteers watching from a post
for the German submarines lurking off the coast.

During the 1940s, the United States was in a bitter war with Germany, known as World War Two. The Germans had a powerful navy including their fleet of "untersee-boots". Unterseeboot means undersea boat in German. They're really just submarines, but U-boats are what German submarines of the 1940s are commonly called.

The U-boats were spread out all over the world during World War Two. Some of them lurked right off the Atlantic coast, waiting to sink American ships or attack American towns. Amelia Island was no exception. Coast Guardsmen sat in the Amelia Island Lighthouse looking for German U-boats in the ocean. Other citizens of Amelia Island volunteered to do the same from the island's beaches.

V is for Victorian, an architectural style
that marks many older homes on this historic isle.
In the late 1800s this style was all the rage.
Now these quaint homes remind us of that age.

Architecture is the science of designing and building homes and other buildings. During Amelia Island's Golden Age of the late 1800s, the Victorian style of architecture was very popular in America. Most of the homes built on the island during this period feature the Queen-Anne variety of Victorian architecture, noted by large wrap-around porches, bay windows, and clapboard siding. A drive through downtown Fernandina can offer you many examples of this style.

W is for worship in the houses where we meet.
Each Sunday morning friends and neighbors take a seat.
Some of these old churches feature stained glass and steeples
that have heard the songs and prayers of many different people.

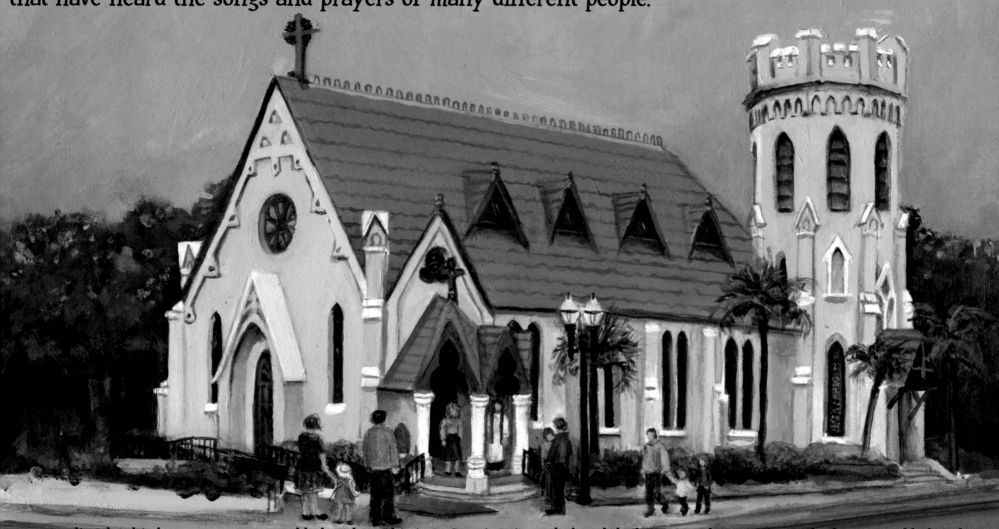

Amelia Island is home to some very old churches. This is St. Peter's Episcopal Church built in 1881. There are several other very old churches in downtown Fernandina like First Presbyterian Church, Macedonia African Methodist Episcopal Church, New Zion Missionary Baptist Church, First Missionary Baptist Church, St. Michael's Roman Catholic Church, Trinity United Methodist Church, and Memorial United Methodist Church. The First Baptist Church was located in downtown Fernandina for a long time but has since moved to South Eighth Street. Other churches on the island have their own special meaning to the people who attend them and have always been very important to life on Amelia Island.

X marks the spot of the hidden pirate's loot
that's rumored to be buried here beside an oak tree's root.
The tree is said to be marked by an old rusty chain,
so keep your eyes peeled if it's treasure you wish to gain.

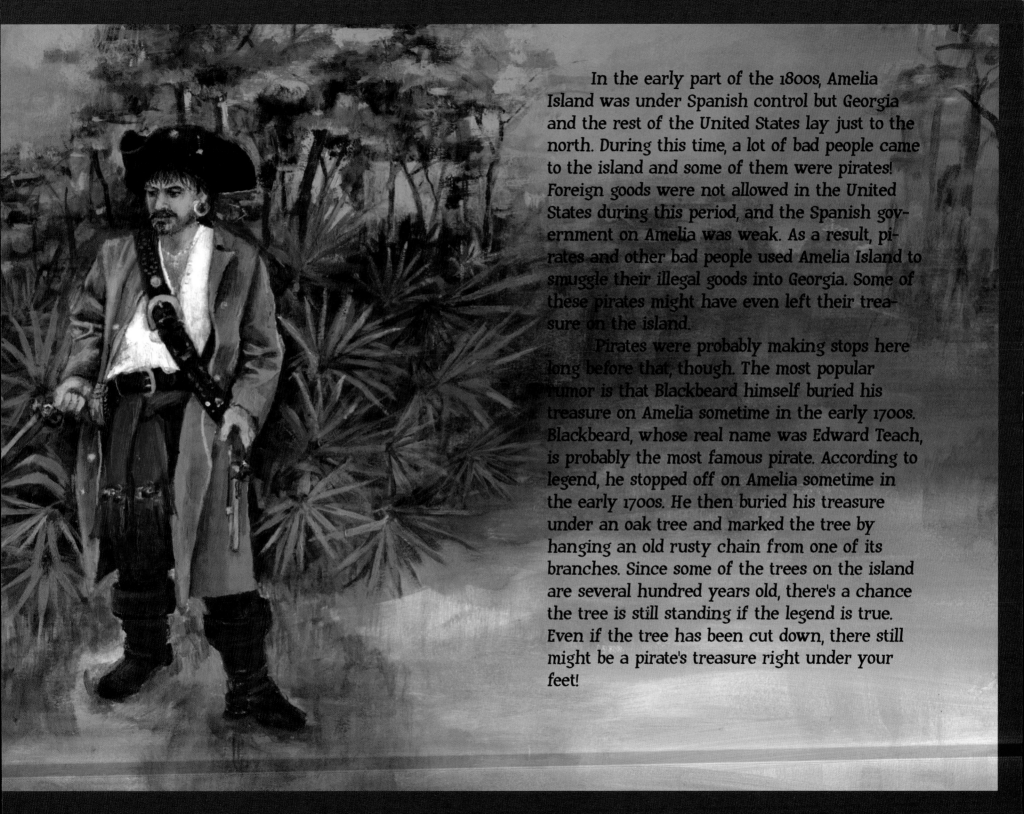

In the early part of the 1800s, Amelia Island was under Spanish control but Georgia and the rest of the United States lay just to the north. During this time, a lot of bad people came to the island and some of them were pirates! Foreign goods were not allowed in the United States during this period, and the Spanish government on Amelia was weak. As a result, pirates and other bad people used Amelia Island to smuggle their illegal goods into Georgia. Some of these pirates might have even left their treasure on the island.

Pirates were probably making stops here long before that, though. The most popular rumor is that Blackbeard himself buried his treasure on Amelia sometime in the early 1700s. Blackbeard, whose real name was Edward Teach, is probably the most famous pirate. According to legend, he stopped off on Amelia sometime in the early 1700s. He then buried his treasure under an oak tree and marked the tree by hanging an old rusty chain from one of its branches. Since some of the trees on the island are several hundred years old, there's a chance the tree is still standing if the legend is true. Even if the tree has been cut down, there still might be a pirate's treasure right under your feet!

Y is for David Yulee, who made Amelia's Golden Age great.
He built the railroad from the island across the state.
Yulee was the first Jewish senator ever in the U.S.
The trains he brought to town gave the economy its zest.

David Yulee is perhaps Amelia Island's most influential person. He was the first Jewish senator in the United States Congress and wrote Florida's state constitution, helping it become a state in 1845.

Yulee had a home on Amelia Island, and in the 1850s he wanted to build a railroad from Fernandina to Cedar Key. This way, goods could be quickly carried across the state and save ships the time and trouble of sailing around the Florida peninsula. His train was called the Florida Railroad. He hoped tourists would use the railroad too, and he built hotels on the island like the Egmont Hotel, the Florida House, and the Strathmore Hotel on the beach. Yulee was a very wealthy man.

Zest will end our trip through Amelia A to Z.
Our historic isle is full of lots to do and see.
For all those who live here and the tourist industry
tiny Amelia Island is a splendor by the sea.

Amelia Island is a wonderful place. Whether you live here or are just visiting you can't help but appreciate all the island has to offer. This little island in the northeast corner of Florida has a deep and rich history. The island has been home to many influential people. Some of them were Native Americans, some politicians; others were just looking for a place their family could enjoy. Animals call the island and the water that surrounds it home also. The marsh and ocean are important habitats for many animals. For the residents that live on Amelia today, industries that manufacture paper or serve the tourists provide jobs. Tourists enjoy the area because of its world class resorts and sporting opportunities. For such a little place, Amelia Island truly is remarkable.